Samuel Kirkland Lothrop

Memorial of the Church in Brattle Square

A discourse preached in the church in Brattle square, on the last Sunday of
its use for public worship, July 30, 1871

Samuel Kirkland Lothrop

Memorial of the Church in Brattle Square
A discourse preached in the church in Brattle square, on the last Sunday of its use for public worship, July 30, 1871

ISBN/EAN: 9783744754651

Printed in Europe, USA, Canada, Australia, Japan

Cover: Foto ©Lupo / pixelio.de

More available books at **www.hansebooks.com**

MEMORIAL

OF THE

CHURCH IN BRATTLE SQUARE.

1871.

Memorial of the Church in Brattle Square.

A

DISCOURSE

PREACHED IN THE CHURCH IN BRATTLE SQUARE,

ON THE

LAST SUNDAY OF ITS USE FOR PUBLIC WORSHIP,

JULY 30, 1871.

BY

SAMUEL K. LOTHROP, D.D.,

PASTOR OF THE SOCIETY.

WITH AN APPENDIX,

AND

AN ACCOUNT OF LAYING THE CORNER-STONE OF THE
NEW CHURCH.

BOSTON:
PRESS OF JOHN WILSON AND SON.
1871.

Rev. Dr. Lothrop.

Dear Sir, — The Standing Committee of the Church and Society in Brattle Square respectfully ask of you a copy of your able and eloquent Sermon, preached on the occasion of holding religious services for the last time in Brattle Square.

The Committee propose to have the Sermon printed in pamphlet form, and to place a copy with the archives of the church.

With the highest considerations of respect and esteem, we remain your friends and servants,

Franklin Haven,	Abram French,
John Gardner,	Chas. Lyman,
J. P. Healy,	Christopher T. Thayer,
Benj. P. Cheney,	T. Quincy Browne,
Eben'r Dale,	O. W. Peabody, and
Geo. W. Palmer,	J. T. Bradlee.

Lewis B. Bailey, *Clerk.*

Boston, Sept. 20, 1871.

To the Standing Committee of the Church and Society worshipping in Brattle Square.

Gentlemen, — Your letter of Aug. 3 received immediate attention after my return from my vacation. I am gratified to find that I met an occasion of so much interest to all of us in a manner satisfactory to my parishioners and friends. From my own notes, and the very full and accurate reports in the newspapers, I have prepared a copy of my Sermon for publication, which I herewith submit to your disposal.

With the highest regard, and many pleasant and grateful recollections, I am, gentlemen, very sincerely your friend and pastor,

S. K. LOTHROP.

DISCOURSE.

"ENLARGE the place of thy tent, and let them stretch forth the curtains of thine habitations, . . . and great shall be the peace of thy children." Thus saith the prophet Isaiah, in this 54th chapter. "Thou shalt worship the Father in spirit and in truth, for the Father seeketh such to worship him." Thus spake the blessed Master, in conversation with the woman of Samaria, recorded in the 4th chapter of St. John's Gospel. Both these scriptures are appropriate mottoes for our thoughts this day, which, though it looks to the future, belongs largely to the past. We meet for the last time on this spot, which, for more than one hundred and seventy years, has been consecrated to the worship of Almighty God. We come to bid farewell for ever to this grand and noble old church, which has stood, for nearly a century, a monument testifying to the faith and piety of our Fathers; and which, to some of us, from our earliest childhood, and to all of us for long, long years, has been the religious home of our souls, full of all tender and sacred associations. Naturally, our thoughts revert to the past ; and to gather up the lessons of that past, as they are presented in the history of this church, in the spirit, purpose, and principles in which it originated, and to which it has ever faithfully adhered, — this becomes at once a grateful pleasure, and a sacred duty.

Any reference to the times, any study of the circumstances under which this church originated, brings up to our thoughts the emphatic declaration of the Master : " Thou shalt worship the Father in spirit and in truth," — a declaration that does not forbid nor denounce nor dispense with forms, but which, while it permits a large liberty in relation to them, does require that they be simple and appropriate; that faith accept them; that the heart vitalize them; and that thus they become a sincere expression of thought and feeling, and help to quicken, enlarge, and invigorate the thought, the feeling, the faith and piety which they are designed to express.

Always in the church, as in all civil and social life, there have been exhibited two opposing tendencies, — the one tendency favoring freedom and simplicity in the forms and administration of religion; the other favoring authority, and more or less of imposing ceremony and ritualistic display. The latter tendency finds its culmination in the Roman Catholic Church, and the former one of its strongest manifestations in that English Puritanism, which, disheartened by persecution and ill success at home, came to New England in the persons of some of its noblest and most devoted disciples, that here it might have freedom, and establish a church without a bishop, and a State without a king; or, rather, that it might establish a church that should be the State, and a State that should be the church. This was the great mistake of early New-England Puritanism, — the point wherein it limited or violated freedom, if not simplicity. Though in many respects grand and glorious, Puritanism was an extreme, overlooking, in the culture and administration of religion, some useful and important elements of human nature which ought never to be disregarded; and, in other respects, adopting various peculiarities, which had little or nothing to recommend them, save that they were the very opposite of prelative usages, to which it was bound by all means not to conform. Puritanism would not use the Lord's Prayer, in public or private, because the " Book of Common Prayer " required its repetition several times in some, and once in all its services. Puritanism would not read the Scriptures in public worship, because the "Book of Common Prayer" required a monthly repetition of the Psalms, and a full and systematic reading of large portions of the Bible, in the course of the year. And, for the same reason, because the "Book of Common Prayer" provided for various chants and singings, Puritanism would sing but once, in any public service. Puritanism neglected altogether the æsthetic element in human nature; and for religious expression, for the quickening of the religious sensibilities, it scorned all use of that sense of the beautiful, the grand, and imposing, to which God constantly appeals, in the solemn magnificence of the universe. A stern, cold, and uninviting simplicity of form and outward service, resting upon nothing, appealing to nothing but the spirit of faith and piety, and appealing to these through logic and argument, rather than the tender and sympathetic elements of our nature, — this was the distinctive, characteristic feature of Puritanism in New England.

But its great mistake was in undertaking to combine the church and State, and confine citizenship, with all its rights and prerogatives, to church members. Such an exclusive and arbitrary rule could not last long. It could only prevail during the lives of the original emigrants, who were all church members, and were moved to voluntary exile for conscience's sake; and as soon as that generation passed, as early as 1662, this disability was removed, and every freeholder became a citizen, with a vote and a voice in all public affairs. But, in ecclesiastical matters, in the management of religious societies and parishes, the church — technically speaking, — the communicants still struggled, first for absolute and exclusive control, and then for the right to take the initiatory steps, and direct the movements of the parish.

Just at this point, we find the germ of this old Brattle-Square Church and Society. It did not originate in any quarrel, nor in any separation from any other church in the town. It did not originate in any dispute or controversy upon points of theological doctrine. Its source was simply a determined purpose, on the part of its founders, to establish a new religious society, in which the Gospel and its ordinances should be administered upon a more liberal and generous plan than then prevailed, imposing exactions upon none, and withholding rights from none. The enterprise met with opposition of such force and character, that " the undertakers," as they were called, just before their first church was dedicated, in November, 1699, put forth a document styled " A Manifesto," in order, as they say, " to prevent misapprehensions and jealousies, and to set forth their designs and aims, and the principles to which, by the grace of God, they meant to adhere." This manifesto contained sixteen articles. The first one is as follows: " We approve and subscribe to the confession of faith put forth by the Assembly of Divines at Westminster." This declaration, of course, shows that upon points of theological doctrine the founders of this church did not assume to differ from the mass of Congregational churches of that time. The points upon which they differed, and thereby gave offence, related to custom and usage in the administration of religion. They were four in number. The first, according to the published manifesto, was, " Reading of the Scriptures in public worship," — a custom largely neglected then among the Puritan Congregationalists in England, and, I believe, absolutely abandoned in this country. " We design only the true and pure worship of God, according as it appears to us from the Holy Scriptures. Therefore, we deem it meet, suitable, and convenient that a portion of the Bible be read always in public worship, at the discretion of the minister." Here was something that savored of a return to prelatic usage; and as it was understood (though not stated in the manifesto) that in the new church the Lord's Prayer was to be repeated once by the minister in the public service every Sunday (a custom which traditionary usage has handed down to the present time), this innovation of reading the Scriptures at public worship was especially offensive to the conservative Puritanism of that day.

The second point related to the proper subjects of baptism, — who were entitled to have it administered to their children? The Independent Congregational churches of England administered baptism only to infants whose parents were church members; but the free air of the wilderness very soon had its effect upon the New-England churches, leading them to abandon many of the customs and usages which they had brought from the Fatherland; and, as early as 1637, letters of inquiry, remonstrance, and entreaty were received from England, cautioning the brethren, and urging adherence to the old paths. For more than half a century after the settlement of New England, the question whether the children of non-church members should be baptized was a subject of controversy, waxing and waning, reviving and subsiding. Some churches satisfied themselves with a half-way covenant, as it was called, by acknowledging which parents could have their children baptized without being or becoming church members themselves. But though this was approved by the synod of 1662, the popular side was the old rule; the majority stood by that. But the course taken by the undertakers of the new church, in Brattle Square, was especially offensive. They did not even establish a "half-way covenant," but threw the whole responsibility upon the parents presenting a child, and upon the minister, who was left to receive such acknowledgments as were satisfactory to himself. "This being a ministerial office, we believe it to be sufficient that the pastor should be satisfied; we leave it to his wisdom and prudence."

So in regard to the third point, — admission to the church. Here, they threw the responsibility entirely upon the candidate seeking admission, and the pastor of the church. "All persons," says the manifesto, "seeking admission should be persons of visible sanctity." "Whoever would be received should be accountable to the pastor, whose duty it is to make himself acquainted with their knowledge and spiritual state. Therefore, we cannot enjoin, we dare not enjoin upon any a public relation of experience. If any person think himself bound in conscience to make such relation, let him do it; but we deem it sufficient if the pastor, by a seasonable announcement of the name of the candidate, indicates that he is satisfied." Here was a very important step. This public relation of experience, before one could be received into the church, was a grievous wrong and oppression, full of evil, and in every way one would think injurious in its influence. It could not but encourage, in some, vanity and self-conceit; it could not but lead others unconsciously into hypocritical, false, or exaggerated statements as to their religious experience; and it necessarily deterred many timid persons from the observance of an ordinance from which they might have derived great comfort and strength, and which should have no barriers thrown around it, except what the Master reared when he said, " Do this, in remembrance of me." Our Fathers did good service, noble service to the cause of religious liberty and sincerity, by discountenancing, as they did, the public relation of experience. They did not feel themselves at liberty to go further. Having no right to enjoin, so they had no right to forbid. " If any person think himself bound, in conscience, to make such relation, let him do it." Thus putting it upon the glorious platform of personal, religious liberty.

The fourth and last point announced in the manifesto, as a principle to which the undertakers of this church designed to adhere, was perhaps the most important in its practical working, and gave most offence to the churches, technically so called; because it took away the prestige that surrounded them, and the authority which they had claimed, exercised, and were still struggling to keep in their own hands. The manifesto says that " persons of the greatest piety, and gravity, and wisdom, and authority, and other accomplishments should, of course, have leading influence and control in the management of our parish affairs; but we cannot confine the right of voting to the church members alone. We hold and maintain that all who contribute to its maintenance should have a vote and voice in election." This, I believe (and I think I have the reliable authority of the late Rev. Dr. Lamson of Dedham, for the statement), was the first instance among the Puritan Congregational churches of New England, in which it was distinctly announced and avowed as a principle to be adhered to and acted upon, that the church — technically speaking — the body of communicants had no rights or powers above those of the congregation. Previously in three instances, one in Salem, one in Dedham, and one in Charlestown — the first in 1672, the second in 1685, and the third in 1697 — by a mutual agreement and provision beforehand, the church and congregation had met together in one body, and without a separate or distinct vote elected their pastor. But this was not the common usage, nor was it the principle avowed and contended for. According to that principle the church had the exclusive right to elect the pastor by a separate and distinct vote, and the right and duty of the congregation was to confirm that vote. They had no power to make a new choice by a separate and

independent vote. This last article in the manifesto sweeping away, as it did, what was regarded
as the special right and prerogative of the church,
or the body of communicants, was particularly
offensive. The Salem ministers, Higginson and
Noyes, who replied to the manifesto, condemn it
" as having a direct tendency to subvert the ministry and grace and order and liberty of all the
churches in the land," and think it " may make
worse work than they care to say." Fortunately
their fears were not realized.

These four points, — 1. Reading of the Scriptures
in public worship; 2. Baptism at the liberty of the
pastor ; 3. Admission to the church without the
public relation of experience ; 4. The extinction
of all special right on the part of the church, and
the recognition of the right of every individual
member of the congregation who contributed to its
support to vote in its affairs, — these constitute the
most essential and important principles which our
Fathers put forth and established in the erection of
this church. I have dwelt upon them at this length
because I felt that. to those of us who knew, it would
be a pleasure to recall them; and I wished that all
who did not know should be made acquainted with
the noble origin and honorable early history of this
church, — the truly Christian spirit, and principle,
and purpose of our Fathers who instituted it. They

were not reckless and conceited disorganizers;
they were not come-outers and radicals, according
to the modern use of these terms. They were men
of solid and substantial Christian faith. They believed in the Bible, and they determined that in the
church which they erected and sustained the Bible
should be read publicly from the pulpit, as the
source and the authority of the truths and instructions which the pulpit uttered. They believed in
the Lord Jesus Christ as the Son of God, anointed
of the Father to be the teacher and Saviour of the
world; and they determined that in their church,
instituted in his name, his Gospel should be so administered that He and not the church should be
the sole Master and Lord of conscience. They
were men of faith, holiness, and prayer, who saw
that a new church was needed in the growing
town, and determined to establish one that should
be liberal yet conservative, uniting freedom and
order, the liberty of the individual with the rights
and progress of the whole body. The points in
which they departed from the usages of the Congregational churches of their day were in one
aspect mere matters of form and administration,
but they involved questions of individual right and
privilege. And we have reason to hold our founders and Fathers in grateful honor and reverence,
that they stood fast in the liberty wherewith Christ

has made us free; and we are not to be surprised, we cannot be surprised, that a church originating in this spirit, founded upon and adhering to these principles should soon have become large and flourishing; or that continuing faithful to them it has been throughout its history a prosperous and peaceful church.

Brethren, I do not propose to dwell thus minutely upon any further details; nor is it necessary, for the later history of this church, and the ministries of Thacher, Buckminster, Everett, and Palfrey are well known and familiar to many who hear me. But I must refer to some of the particulars connected with the first two pastors. The first movement in relation to this religious society was made in 1697. In January, 1698, the undertakers became possessed of a lot of land in Brattle Close, but for some reason which cannot be ascertained they took no steps toward erecting a house of worship until the spring of 1699. In a letter dated the 10th of May of that year, addressed to Mr. Coleman, in England, inviting him to become their pastor, they say: "The timber for our church has already been brought to town; the frame will be raised the first of August, and the house completed in October." A simple wooden structure, that was thus to be built in the course of three or four months, could not, manifestly, have been a very elaborate structure.

But in that humble temple, Dr. Coleman, for nearly forty-eight years, preached and labored with a wisdom, a fidelity, and success that have seldom been surpassed. He was a native of this town, and his brother was one of the " undertakers " of this church. He graduated at Harvard College in 1692; and, after delivering the master's oration, travelled, studied and preached in England about four years; and at the moment this invitation from Boston reached him he was preaching to a distinguished dissenting congregation in Bath. Having determined to accept it, and anticipating from the state of things here that there might be difficulty in obtaining ordination in Boston, he proceeded to London, and there on the 4th of August, 1699, he was ordained as the pastor of this church by some of the most distinguished dissenting clergymen of that city. He arrived here on the 1st of November, 1699, and in a very few weeks he and the people of his church were quietly worshipping God according to their consciences in their new and simple church. In a very few years the relations of Dr. Coleman and his society with the other ministers and churches in the town became pleasant and harmonious, and the distinctions and the title, " manifesto," which first marked and separated the church in Brattle Square, were obliterated by the adoption by most of the Congregational churches of New England of the principles, customs, and usages which that church had introduced. It was a blessed providence that led to the choice of Dr. Coleman to be the first minister of this church. Among the men of his day there was no one who had so large a measure of the requisite combination of qualities for the difficult post. Had he and his people resembled many pastors and societies of the present day, — who seem to be zealous for all manner of useless and unnecessary innovations, and anxious to hold out the idea that there is something very peculiar in their society, their modes and methods of administering the Gospel, — they might have made at that early day a fatal schism in the Congregational churches of the colony. But he was for peace and conciliation. He was anxious, so far as it could be done without a compromise of dignity and principle, to keep his church in union and harmony, not in contrast and conflict, with the other churches in town. By wisdom, firmness, and gentleness he succeeded to the content of his heart; and in 1747, when he died, it would be difficult to name one who, as an accomplished scholar, a courteous Christian gentleman, a wise, faithful, earnest, eloquent preacher, a devoted and attentive pastor, an honest, patriotic, public-spirited citizen, had rendered more important service to the community, or was held in higher regard by all the churches in Massachusetts, than Benjamin Coleman, the first pastor of Brattle-Square Church.

He had two colleagues, — the Rev. William Cooper, who was ordained on the 23d of May, 1716, and, after twenty-seven years of associated labor, died on the 14th of December, 1743, leaving Dr. Coleman, in his advanced age, the sole pastor of the church,— a charge from which he was presently relieved by the choice of a son of William Cooper, the Rev. Samuel Cooper, to be associate pastor. He was ordained on the 22d of May, 1746, just sixteen months before the death of Dr. Coleman, after which, for thirty-seven years, till his own death, in December, 1783, he was the sole pastor of the church. These two pastorates of Coleman and Cooper cover nearly one-half the period that has elapsed since the organization of the church. Dr. Cooper is better known to us by tradition than Dr. Coleman. He was an accomplished gentleman and scholar, dignified and imposing in personal presence, an eloquent preacher, and faithful pastor, and also a man of affairs, — taking a deep interest in, and in various ways exercising a large influence upon all the public questions and events of that stormy period between 1750 and 1783, when he died.

From his pastorate Brattle-Square Church becomes a distinct and tangible reality to us of this generation; for then was erected this splendid temple of worship, which, in its substantial structure, in the grand and imposing solemnity of its interior, has not been equalled, certainly not surpassed, by any church that the Protestant faith has since erected in the city of the Pilgrims. It was formerly thought, and has been sometimes pretty strongly asserted, that, after the great awakening of 1740, a period of coldness and deadness came upon the New-England churches, which was increased and prolonged, made deeper and darker through the political troubles of the times, — the French war and the war of the Revolution, — and that during the last half of the last century there was very little manifestation of a living, vigorous religious faith in these churches. We are beginning to correct this idea, and do a little more justice to that period. We ought to correct our estimate; for surely the people who resisted the Stamp Act and the Boston Port bill, and held the principles that inaugurated the revolution of 1776, and who carried their country triumphantly through that great struggle, could not have been an irreligious people, nor largely wanting in that religious faith which is truly the inspiration of the noblest and most honorable action in all our political and public affairs.

But, whatever may have been the general spiritual state, we may rightfully claim that this church

of our Fathers, in 1770, was in good condition
spiritually and materially. They must have been
and felt themselves strong materially; for, when
they were about to build this church, they refused
the offered gift of a most eligible lot of land of far
greater value than this which they held, — a lot
worth thousands then, worth hundreds on hundreds
of thousands to-day, — and refused partly because
they did not want to leave the old spot, and partly
because the majority of the parish lived immediately north of the church, and Brattle Close was very
accessible to them. They purchased more land
here, and then raised, by voluntary subscription
among themselves, twenty thousand pounds lawful
money, — equivalent, I suppose, to more than
$150,000 at the present day, — and erected this
grand and substantial church, which, untouched by
hand of man, would defy for centuries the inroads
of time. We need no better evidence, brethren,
of the faith of our Fathers; that a good spirit was
in them, and an efficient ministry at work among
them. This church could not have been built
without faith, or without that generous devotion to
the honor of God and the good of man which faith
inspires. And in comparison with similar work in
our times, it was very speedily built. The society
worshipped for the last time in the old wooden
church on this spot, the 10th of May, 1772. The

corner-stone of this church was laid on the 23d
June, 1772. The church itself was finished, dedicated and worshipped in by our Fathers on the
25th of July, 1773, — ninety-eight years ago last
Wednesday, and about thirteen months from the
time its corner-stone was laid. Is there a con-
tractor or master mechanic among us to-day who
would undertake to build this church, with its thick
massive walls and all the noble carved work of its
interior, in the time in which the mechanics and
workmen of Boston erected it nearly one hundred
years ago?

But the society was not permitted long to enjoy
it unmolested. As we know, the troubles of the
Revolution came on; and Dr. Cooper, whose patriotic sermons, services, and character made him
obnoxious to the royal authorities, left the town in
April, 1775, and did not return until after the siege.
The services were suspended when the siege com-
menced ; the military commandant wanted the
church for military purposes, and made it a barrack. The patriot enemy fired upon it from without,
and struck it; the British soldiers within marred
and defaced it with their bayonets, and left it in
such a condition that several weeks elapsed after
the evacuation by the British forces before it could
be used for the purposes for which it was erected,
— the public worship of God. But these circum-

stances caused it, before it was a decade old, to become an historic church, around which patriotic memories and associations soon gathered, and have since been increasing, strengthening, and over-flowing with every generation; so that now it is a matter of regret, not simply to the worshippers in this church, but to the great body of our citizens generally, that this noble and glorious old edifice, this splendid landmark of the past, should pass away.

That regret is natural and right. I should feel little respect for any man who did not share in it. No one can feel it more sadly or deeply than myself. My ministry covers more than one-third of the time since this church was erected. I have preached from this pulpit nearly twenty years longer than any of my predecessors; and, however little it may be, nearly all that there is of honor or usefulness in my professional life is associated with this spot. If ever I have felt an hour of triumphant satisfaction, — perhaps it was a weakness to indulge in it, — at the thought of work well done, duty faith-fully discharged, it has been when, standing here, looking into the faces of parishioners and friends, I have led their devotions, set forth the teachings, hopes, promises of the Gospel, and uttered, as best I could, the truths that pertain to their own welfare and to the highest interests of humanity. For more than thirty years these majestic columns have flanked me on either side, like grand and solemn sentinels, keeping silent watch and ward over this pulpit which, with its sacred memories, traditions, and associations, has been my inspiration and my throne. The thought of leaving all this glory, of departing from it and seeing it depart, makes my heart throb; nay, makes every fibre of my frame quiver with deep and sad emotions.

So is it with you, brethren, members of this society, worshippers in Brattle-Square Church. I can understand and sympathize with all the feelings that arise in your hearts this day at the thought of leaving this home of your religious affections, this scene, perhaps, of your deepest religious experience, connected so intimately with all the joy and all the sorrow of your lives. Sad and sacred, holy and hallowed memories gather around it in your minds; nay, with some of you, who are even now near the close of life, the recollections of early childhood cluster thick and fast about it this morning. In unconscious infancy you were baptized at this altar. Hither the hand of parental affection early led your childhood's steps to the worship of God; and through all the years of life the path has been familiar to your feet, and even now is sweet and pleasant through the memory of the parents, brothers, sisters, who once trod it with you, but long since, it may be, have passed from your sight, and left you to tread it alone.

But where recollection goes not back to early childhood, it goes back, with many of you, to the dawn of early manhood, when stepping upon the stage of life you rested here the ark of your faith, made this the tabernacle of your worship, sought here the truths that were to guide and the influences that were to protect you amid all the duty and peril of life. And through all that duty and peril, through prosperous and adverse fortunes, your hearts weary with the heavy burden of sorrow, or glad with gratitude and praise, hither you have come, Sunday after Sunday, year after year, and found strength and comfort, the Master's peace and a spiritual benediction on your soul. And now, to-day, to you who are here present, as to many who are not present, to many scattered all over the land, ay, and in foreign lands, the thought of this church comes up to the memory like a golden thread of light and love and comfort, of hope and strength, woven into the very texture of your hearts, an inseparable portion of the warp and woof of your being; and to cut that thread, to drift away from this spot, so familiar, sacred, dear to all that is noblest and best in your souls, and see all this material glory and beauty depart, — this begets in your hearts a sadness that may be almost called a bitterness of spirit.

Yes, friends, it is natural, it is right, that we should feel deep sorrow and regret at leaving this noble old church; but we should not indulge this feeling until it becomes morbid and deaf to all the suggestions of wisdom and sound judgment. We should not indulge it until it paralyze effort and make us forget what we owe to the future in return for what we have received from the past. Change is the order of Divine Providence; nothing is permanent or enduring upon earth but truth and duty, and these vary in the efforts and sacrifices they demand of us, with the varying circumstances in which we are placed. Reduced to the last analysis, the question which has been for some years before us was simply a question of conscience and of duty rather than of feeling. "Shall this old church and society in Brattle Square remain on the spot where it was born, and die there; or shall it remove to another site, and, carrying with it its traditions and its history, seek to perpetuate itself as a religious organization, and go down into the coming generations a living power and not a lifeless memory that must soon become utterly and for ever extinct?" That this was the question, the simple alternative, can, I think, neither be doubted nor denied. You have felt it, and I have felt it. The history and experience of similar institutions in all large and growing cities in this country and in

Europe confirm it by unequivocal testimony.
There are grand traditions and histories connected
with this church, and it is an imposing, impressive
old building; but it is so unpleasantly situated, the
access to it from every direction has for the last
twenty years been so disagreeable, and will so unquestionably become more and more unpleasant,
that the mightiest voice that ever uttered itself
in a Christian pulpit, — and such voice is not
easily obtained, nor does it live for ever if obtained, — could not, I apprehend, keep this church
alive on this spot for a quarter of a century longer. It was not meet that we should abide here
for the gratification of our personal feelings of
attachment and reverence for this spot and this
house, and leave the religious organization trans-
mitted to us from the Fathers, the living church of
living and immortal souls, to perish and die out.
To preserve and perpetuate the religious organization, and send it down into the community and the
generations to come after us, — this was the more
sacred, imperative and Christian duty, to be discharged at whatever sacrifice of our personal feelings and affections, at whatever cost to our personal
comfort.

And we have not been hasty in this matter, my
friends. Some may think that we have delayed too
long, but assuredly we have not been hasty. It is

now full twenty-five years since the first distinct
proposition for a change of location was made to
the society by several gentlemen, all but one of
whom have since died. Those gentlemen held at
that time the refusal of the estate where the Music
Hall now stands, and the question of removal, with
that estate in prospect, was brought to a distinct
vote in the society, and decided in the negative by
a very large majority. In the providence of God
the time had not come. But during the twenty-five
years since elapsed, the question has been a constant
subject of thought and discussion in the parish, and,
once or twice, of some pretty direct practical efforts
on the part of the standing committee, and four or
five years have passed since the measures that are
now issuing in our removal were instituted. They
have been pressed gently and gradually on the
parish. We have not been hasty; we have moved
slowly, because we wished that every thing should
be done, as every thing in the past history of the
church has been done, in peace and harmony, in as
near an approach to unanimity as possible. Time
has been allowed for a full interchange of opinions,
for wisdom and judgment to temper the natural im-
pulses of feeling, of affection, and attachment; until
now I believe there is all but a universal concurrence among the worshippers in this church and
among our citizens generally, who feel that they

have, as it were, some right of property in this old
landmark of the past, — there is everywhere an
almost universal concurrence in the proposition
that Brattle-Square Church and Society must remove, if they would live.

The hard necessity of the first part of this alternative is forced upon us in the providence of God
by the growth and prosperity of the city. The
fulfilment of the last part of it — perpetuating our
life — depends, under the providence of God, upon
ourselves. That is a question to be determined
by the fidelity of our own hearts to duty and principle. The necessity of removal being admitted,
the removal itself determined upon, just in propor-
tion to the measure of our attachment to this spot
and to this church, with all its history and traditions, should be the energy of our efforts to transfer
it, with this history and these traditions, — the real
church, the living spiritual church, — to the new
spot, and there build it up. And why should we
not do this? Are our religious feelings and associations so much more local and confined than those
of every other part of our nature, that we cannot
meet the changes that require us to transfer them
to new scenes? Is our worship such a formal affair,
so dependent upon the influence of outward and
accustomed surroundings, that we cannot compre-
hend and feel, act upon and obey, that grand dec-

laration of the Master, " Thou shalt worship the Father in spirit and in truth, for the Father seeketh such to worship him"? No, brethren: that spiritual worship of the heart we can carry everywhere; and it is in our power, by forbearance, by tenderness, by an earnest, concurrent zeal, to carry out — nay, we shall carry out to a glorious and noble conclusion — the goodly enterprise upon which we have now entered. We shall " enlarge the place of our tent; " we " shall stretch forth the curtains of our new habitation, and great will be the peace of our children."

Every thing is favorable for us if our own hearts are full of courage and hope, of forbearance and faith. Through the kindness of one of the oldest and most honored churches in this city, in offering for our use their chapel in Freeman Place, Beacon Street, comfortable provisions have been made for our worship until our new church shall be ready for our reception. Let us gratefully go there, and cleave together and cling together in work and love. I presume not to dictate; I interfere not with the liberty which any family or individual may choose to exercise upon this subject: no one will accuse me of any professional arrogance of that sort; but in the name of the blessed Master, whose truth we have sought together to uphold here; in the name of those great and precious interests which for more

than thirty years I have stood here to defend and
advance as best I could; by all the blessed memories and associations of the past, — I do entreat you,
even those who have least favored the enterprise
now begun, and say to you, let us cleave together
and cling together and work together with loving
· hearts, with living faith, with earnest efforts; and
then those efforts shall be crowned with success,
and the glory of the latter house shall exceed the
former, and the blessing of God will rest upon us
and upon our children even as it did upon our
Fathers.

Nothing remains for us now, brethren, but to take
leave of this dear, blessed, familiar spot. Farewell,
then, for ever, thou grand, glorious, blessed old
church! An earnest faith and a devout piety laid
thy foundations, reared thy walls, planted thy
columns, adorned thy pulpit, and made thee a grave
and goodly house of worship. Earnest, learned,
faithful and eloquent men, preachers and pastors,
have stood in thy pulpit, and made thy walls re-
sound with utterances of sacred and divine truth,
with appeals to the heart and the conscience that
could not be resisted. Successive generations of
wise, good, devout, patriotic, Christian men and
women of high or low, humble or exalted station,
have filled thy pews and drunk from thy fountain of
living waters the influences that have been the com-

fort and joy of their hearts, that have made them useful and happy upon earth and meet for heaven. Through all thy worshippers, in successive generations, thou hast connected thyself directly with much that is patriotic, useful, noble, honorable and of good report in this community. But thy mission is done, thy work is accomplished, thy office fulfilled. The mandate to depart is issued, and we leave thee now for ever. But we will not forget thee. Thine image, holy and beautiful, of mingled grandeur, grace, and dignity, shall abide for ever in our hearts, a blessed memory, a quickening inspiration. Often we will recall thee; and when our hearts have ceased to beat upon earth, and no one of the living generations can say, "I remember thee," even then thy fame shall survive: and in the great communion of the saints, multitudes worshipping in temples not made with hands, eternal in the heavens, shall there look back, and remember thee with gratitude and reverence, as the spot where their hearts were born to Christ, and their souls made meet for glory and honor and immortality. Farewell for ever, noble, glorious, blessed old church in Brattle Square!

APPENDIX.

—

THE removal of an old historic landmark, like Brattle-Square Church, was an event of too much general interest and importance for the public press of the city to permit it to pass unnoticed. The whole of the foregoing Sermon, reported with singular correctness, appeared in several newspapers on the Monday morning after its delivery, with glowing and elaborate descriptions of the scene and service at the church in some of them, and with kind and friendly comment in all. One or two interesting and noteworthy articles also, on "the Manifesto Church," and its contemplated removal, were published on the Saturday previous, July 29. As these articles are expressions or indications of the public opinion and feeling of the time, and thus, while interesting to all, are especially interesting to the members of Brattle-Square Society, and may be needed or desired in some convenient form for historical reference, the Standing Committee have thought it best to reprint some of them in connection with the Society's issue of the Sermon itself.

The following is from the "Daily Advertiser" of Saturday, July 29 : —

THE CHURCH IN BRATTLE SQUARE. — Appropriate religious services at the church in Brattle Square will mark to-morrow one more of the changes which remove the memorials of old Boston. Such changes show us how different is the city of to-day from the little town to which our Fathers gave a reputation honorable the world over. It is nearly two hundred years since the first church was built on the spot which is now surrendered, after a loyal struggle, to the invasion of commerce. The history of the church then established has been honorable, and it has been closely connected with the fortunes of the town and the changing phases of the religious life of New England. We suppose, indeed, that the foundation of this church is, in our local history, the mark which indicates the advance in culture and individual right which in three generations the children of New England had made upon their ancestors. At the end of the seventeenth century the colony was no longer poor, and Boston was no longer a little fishing-town struggling for a right to be. The people who lived in it were no longer new settlers in a wilderness. They had had no home but New England, and they wanted none better. In every regard, therefore, their circumstances differed from those of the first Winthrop, the first Dudley, and their associates; and, however sad the confession to the men who loved to praise the olden time, it was natural that the difference between the first generation and the third should express itself in the forms of their worship.

Mr. Haven has pointed out the curious fact that the second generation was undoubtedly of less culture, literary and religious, than that whose place it took. The infant college could not train such scholars as did Emmanuel and Pembroke and the other tried colleges of the old Cambridge. And the struggles of a wilderness were not the best schools for such culture. But, as prosperity increased, as wealth increased, here in the metropolis especially, small though the metropolis was, culture asserted its own again. The elegancies of life came in with the other prizes of commerce; and it is evident that the literary, scientific, and religious tastes and studies of the generation that grew up as the century came to an end were no longer those of an insignificant fishing-town.

It is as evident that the closely-serried power of the early Puritan church could not hold its own in a community where that church no longer dreaded the arm of persecution. Blaxton had said, as early as 1638, that he found the Lord's brethren masters as hard as any lord bishop. It was not in the nature of New England to bear indefinitely any close screws, whether imposed by a congregational or a prelatical star-chamber. And it was therefore inevitable that so soon as the church of the colonies was sure of freedom from persecution, it would, as its elastic constitution permitted so readily, assert its freedom from theological dictation.

Each tendency of advance — whether in literary and theological culture, whether in freedom of expression, or whether in liberty of thought — was in a quiet way exemplified in the establishment of the church in Brattle Square. The "Manifesto Church," it was called in its day, — being indeed the "Protestant" church among the Puritan congregations. It did not separate from their fellowship ; but it instituted novelties in worship which at the time were considered extraordinary, and which were sufficient to denote the real independency of the congregation. To the observer of to-day, looking back upon these changes, they appear singularly small. That the Bible should always be read in the conduct of divine service was one of them. The true Puritan carried his dread of book-worship so far, that this was a novelty. That the Lord's prayer should be used in every service was one of the early customs, which became traditional in this church. The older Puritans had dreaded such an approach to a form. Most remarkable of all was the permission given to each person who wished to join in the communion of the church, to make to the pastor his own statement of religious experience in private, — and the waiver of the old custom of a public proclamation of such experience. In this last concession is to be found the recognition and consecration by the "Manifesto Church" of the right of private judgment. These changes in ritual seem to us very small. They indicate, however, the determination on the part of the most intelligent and influential of the laity of the town of Boston, as it then was, to keep in their own hands the direction of the methods of public worship, — their determination to have it conducted in such way as to meet best their own wishes and necessities, — and their refusal to submit in such matters to the notions of the coteries of the clergy. The establishment of the "Manifesto Church" may be said to show that Boston was no longer governed by a hierarchy, if indeed it had ever been.

It is needless to say that the church founded on such a principle has always furnished distinguished illustrations of its value. The church in Brattle Square united, through the century which followed its formation, a large number of those citizens of this town who were most closely connected with the administration of public affairs. To this time the "convention of the clergy," which is the Massachusetts "convocation," holds its annual religious service in this church. In the services of the Colmans, of the Coopers, and of Thacher in its pulpit, it maintained the claim which the manifesto made for the fit illustration of sacred learning by the best studies of modern literature and science, and for the true consecration of the thought of the time by the lessons of sacred learning. The names of Buckminster and Everett, and of their successors still living, are enough to show that in this century it has not been false to the same mission.

This church stood for individual liberty in contrast to the pressure of a congregation, and for modern culture in the place of traditional ritual or theology. There was therefore, of course, no question where it would be found, when the religious discussions of the earlier part of this century divided the Congregational communion of Massachusetts. It would be hard, perhaps, to name four men associated together who have done more service to the liberal communion of Congregationalists than have the four men who successively filled the pulpit of this church since that discussion began. For eloquence, for scholarship, for critical knowledge of Scripture, the names of Buckminster, Everett, and Palfrey have been pre-eminent in the

Unitarian communion. And that body, in the organization of its missions and the supervision of its associated action, has had no officer who has served it with more distinction or ability than the present pastor in the years when he was president of its missionary association.

The church, which stood once at the southern end of the fashionable quarter of the town, has long since been far north of the homes of its worshippers. To-morrow they meet for the last time beneath the roof consecrated by so many memories. The building — erected by a pupil of Wren's, in an architecture not unworthy of the school from which it sprung — is to be destroyed. The congregation will carry to their new home some memorials of the old. The cannon-ball which struck the tower when the "rebels" of 1775 fired on the town will be placed in the new tower. The new church, like the old, is to

"Bear on her bosom, as a bride might do,
The iron breast-pin that the rebels threw."

The stately mahogany pulpit, of the best work of the London taste of a century ago, will be removed also. The bell, long the heaviest in Boston, will call together the worshippers. And we trust that the corner-stone, from which the English soldiery hacked the hated name of John Hancock, may be the head-stone of the new corner.

Will it not be possible, as a new square of buildings grow up around the newly built church, to give to it Brattle's name? — that, in the emigration from north to south, the "Manifesto Church" may still stand in Brattle Square.

The "Daily Evening Transcript" of Saturday called attention to the services to be held the next day, in the following sympathetic and commendatory notice : —

"THE MANIFESTO CHURCH" — such as it was originally called, for protesting against some Puritan usages, and introducing marked innovations in the direction of freedom — will

hold its last services to-morrow in the old Brattle Street (we
say old, for there has been an intimation that the new site may
retain the ancient name). The day can hardly fail to be one
of deeply interesting historical reminiscences and memorials
covering a century and three quarters. The story of this consecrated building, so imposing and solid in its architecture, and
its more humble predecessor, has been so frequently told that
it is a familiar chapter in the annals of Boston and New England. But those annals will fail to record the unwritten, and
many of them unspoken, solemn, and tender memories and
associations connected with the ancient tabernacles. These
have been known only to individual experiences. The sacred
uses to which the noble building has been put through scores
of years, the long line of eminent and eloquent preachers that
have discoursed of Christian truth and hope beneath its roof,
have given it a name and a fame unrivalled by any other church
in the land, and hence the significance of the farewell.

Rev. SAMUEL K. LOTHROP, D. D., has already been the
devoted, respected, and beloved pastor of the Brattle-Street
Society for thirty-seven years. And as he takes leave of the
pulpit from which he has so long spoken, hosts of friends will
desire for him, in the health and strength of his veteran powers,
many added seasons of the faithfulness to his immediate charge
and the unwearied practical regard for the best interests of
Boston he has so constantly and signally manifested.

In its issue of Monday, in addition to the report of the
Sermon in its columns, the "Transcript" had another
pleasant notice of the occasion and the services at the
church : —

BRATTLE-STREET CHURCH. — The services of yesterday,
the last Sunday of public worship in that consecrated edifice,
are quite fully reported on the first page. No printed account,
however, will give their impressive significance, as that was
felt by the great congregation present. Several causes com-
bined to make it an event of unusual interest. Associations,

connected with grave questions of religious and civil liberty, have made the name of the structure historic; whilst as a Christian tabernacle, in its succession of pastors and generations of parishioners, its story, written and unwritten, is crowded with the profoundest experience of the human lot and the human life; as these have invoked the truths, the hopes, and the aspirations of that faith which seeks to reconcile this lot and life with the spirit's immortal progress.

No wonder then that, notwithstanding the unpropitious season of the year, the gathering filled every pew and almost packed the aisles. No wonder the sons and daughters of the church — their church, or the church of their fathers — came, as many did, from far and near, to join in exercises of a solemn leave-taking. Thus a natural public interest in an hour overflowing with suggestion was largely supplemented by the strictly personal feelings of individuals and home-circles.

As was fitting, Rev. Dr. LOTHROP was assisted by some of his younger brethren who had gone from beneath its roof to become dispensers of the Christian truth to which they had there first listened. His own discourse, connected with services imposing for their severe simplicity, and what may be called, for that reason, their traditional appropriateness, was in all respects suitable and effective. With brief passages of lucid explanation, and condensed references to the annals of the past, the preacher resisted the temptation to explore anew the rich field those annals presented, and kept himself and his audience to the religious sentiments which the parting hour awoke and for which it demanded expression.

His manly words were eloquent and tender, abounding in reverence for the former days, meeting the obligations of the present, looking hopefully forward to the future; thus setting forth in just relations the changes that must need be with the reminiscences clinging to them, the lessons taught and the responsibilities imposed as the centuries flow irresistibly onward. To the fine apostrophe, so condensed, and yet so warm with subdued emotion, which closed the discourse, not a syllable can be added. The audience present accepted it, and those who read it will do the same, as just the farewell that was to be uttered to interpret the occasion.

The "Christian Register," in its number for Aug. 5, has an article, — "Old Landmarks Removed," — referring to and suggested by the farewell service at Brattle Street : —

THE OLD LANDMARKS GOING. — The services at Brattle Square last Sunday, a report of which, together with Dr. LOTHROP'S Sermon, occupies so large a space in our columns, remind us forcibly of the changes which are taking place in Boston. For the last few years nearly all of the older churches have been on a stampede after their worshippers. The trade of the city having driven the old Bostonians out of their family mansions, and left the churches surrounded with stores, the next step of necessity has been the moving of the churches, so that soon the Old South will be the only reminder, in the heart of the city, of the church edifices of a former generation. The Federal-Street, the New South, the First Church, the Baptist Church on Chauncy Street, Rev. Dr. Adams's on Essex Street, the Catholic Church on Franklin Street, the Winter-Street, — all have taken up their line of march to the newer parts of the city. The Universalist Church in School Street, the Second Church in Bedford, Trinity in Summer, and the old church in Brattle Square, will soon give way for stately stores, and the places where they stood for generations will know them no more.

But these changes mark the transitions of church polity and religious opinions as distinctly as the increase of the city in trade and the moving of the people. The sermon of Dr. LOTHROP illustrates this. "The Manifesto," when written, contained statements of principles, and recommendations of changes, which were regarded as somewhat startling innovations. Now both the practices and principles there set forth have become established in our churches.

Brattle Square is, moreover, specially dear to the Bostonians from the many old and dear memories with which it is associated. It has had a ministry of eminent scholarship and pulpit gifts. There were Colman, Cooper, and Thacher of a former generation. It was here that Buckminster, " the seraph of the pulpit," thrilled the hearts of his hearers by an eloquence as novel as it was fervent and glowing. It was here that Everett began that career as a public speaker, which, in another sphere, has given a grace and charm to American oratory. It was here that Palfrey, with careful scholarship and conscientious fidelity, entered upon pulpit labors, which afterwards ripened into the professor and historian. Its present minister has had a long and faithful pastorate, and is widely known for his pulpit eloquence, and the various public services which he has performed with so great acceptance and ability.

Then, too, the edifice itself is rich in associations. It is connected with the struggles and the memories of the Revolution. It bears the handiwork of one who has, by his genius in church designs, left an imperishable name. But though thus rich in sacred association, this church must yield to the changes of time. The Boston of a former generation, with its cluster of churches, has become a great centre of trade. The old citizens, one by one, have been forced to give up their homes and churches for stores. This is one of the consequences of the increase of Boston. But the city has only entered upon her new enlargement. She is pushing out in every quarter. The future is rich with the promise of added wealth, population, and trade. Will Boston, as she thus is favored with material prosperity, maintain the higher interests of culture and religion? Will this city be the abode of scholars and artists who will throw the light of their influence and genius over literature and social life? Will our ministers, uniting reverence and love of freedom, resist the present temptation to superficial brilliancy, and by earnest and profound study work to advance the progress of Christian truth, and strive to build up churches which shall be both sentinels and lights to watch the public morals and brighten the pathway of progress? In the future we hope to see Boston maintain that foremost position in culture, education, and religion for which she has heretofore been distinguished.

The "Boston Post," of Monday, July 31, had a very full description of the whole scene and service at the church; and its reporter, adhering to facts, but holding a rhetorical pen, gave such play to feeling and imagination as to present a very vivid picture. From his description we make the following extracts : —

THE SERVICES YESTERDAY. — Yesterday morning services were held in the time-honored edifice for the last time. The weather was cloudy and threatening, but not sufficiently so to deter those who would come from coming ; . . . and a most unusual, but under the circumstances perfectly natural, interest was manifested in the event. It was no common one that of taking leave of such a place as Brattle-Street Church. There were many moist eyes to be seen amongst the congregation. There were many old niches looked into for a parting thought. There was a historic fact to many attaching to every window and every pillar, and the pulpit and the organ spoke volumes. . . . There, in 1775, had stood a stack of arms. By that window an officer had hacked at the queer old carvings, and the marks of his sabre are to be seen there still. There, by the pulpit, had been grouped the flags of Great Britain. Around, everywhere, had been scattered the cots of the soldiery. One could trace the precise spot back of where the cannon-ball had struck, and imagine what consternation reigned in the barrack when from the line of the American fortifications the shot was fast dropping into the Square, and the dismal portents of a driving rain-storm filled the air. Thoughts such as these recurred to one sitting in the church while the congregation was coming in, and there was plenty of time to reflect.

At half-past ten o'clock the organist, Mr. I. I. HARWOOD, seated himself before the sacred instrument and played an appropriate prelude. . . . By this time the church was crowded to overflowing. The pews, the galleries, the aisles, the doorways, were filled completely. There was no room for more, and it all went to prove that the traditions of the old edifice are not yet quite forgotten, and that they will not soon be. From the galleries, to one looking down into the body of the church, the scene was deeply impressive. The sturdy array of pillars on either side, the antique mouldings, the pews panelled in green, the brocatelle curtains on the brass rods around the galleries, the curiously shaped windows and the wide sills, the heavy green blinds through which the daylight found its way in a subdued form and fell upon the upturned faces and touched them all and every thing with a hallowed tint, and the worn and faded furnishings were such as to fill a stranger with thoughts akin to sadness in remembrance of the occasion. In the pulpit sat Dr. Lotiirop, . . . by his side the Rev. E. E. Hale. On the table in front were a few flowers, and at each end of the large Bible was a bouquet of beautiful exotics. . . .

After some further description of the scene and the services, and a full report of the Sermon, the " Post " closes with the following reference to—

The Music.—The musical portion of the exercises calls for more than a mere passing mention. The selections were all in the best taste possible, and were performed with remarkably fine effect. The organ, though nearly one hundred years old, has lost none of that purity and rotundity of tone for which it has long been famous, and yesterday it seemed to be conscious of the peculiar solemnity of the day, so grand and beautiful were the effects educed from it. It will be of interest to state, in passing, that it is probable that a large part of the old organ will be recast and incorporated in the new one. Beside the organist, the choir consisted of Mrs. I. I. Harwood, soprano ; Mrs. J. Rametti, alto ; Mr. D. W. Loring, tenor ; and Mr. C. E. Pickett, bass ; and this quartette was assisted in the chorus passages by Mrs. Tower, soprano, and Mr. Garrett, bass, both former members of the choir. Mr. and Mrs. Harwood came to the city from York, Maine, where they were passing a summer vacation, for the express purpose of being present at, and attending to the music of, these farewell services. The selections consisted of an opening quartette from T. Sterndale Bennett's oratorio, "The Woman of Samaria;" "God is a Spirit," sung without the organ; a Gloria, "Now unto the King Eternal," following the reading of the Scriptures; the hymn, "While Thee I seek, Protecting Power," sung to the celebrated and beautiful tune, "Brattle Street," by Pleyel; a Chant, "O Sing unto the Lord," by James Turle; and the concluding Doxology, "From all that dwell below the skies," sung to Old Hundred. The voices of the singers blended perfectly, and the execution of the various tunes and anthems was highly artistic and deserving of unstinted praise. Mr. Harwood handled the organ with appreciative and exceptional skill. Mrs. Harwood's voice is a clear, high and ringing soprano, equally good in each of the registers, while Mrs. Rametti possesses a contralto of remarkable sweetness. Mr. Loring's tenor and Mr. Pickett's bass are also conspicuously excellent, and the whole choir may rightfully congratulate itself upon having achieved a genuine musical triumph, despite the very unfavorable condition of the weather.

It will be long before the last services in the old church in Brattle Square will be forgotten.

The "Post's" reference to the music, and criticism of it, are altogether appropriate and just, and, as an interesting addition and close to it, we publish what to some is a well-known and unquestionably authentic tradition in Brattle-Square Church, in regard to the hymn, "While Thee I seek, Protecting Power," and the tune, "Brattle Street," to which it is almost invariably sung. When Rev. Mr. Buckminster returned from Europe in 1807, he brought with him a manuscript copy of this hymn, presented to him by its celebrated author, Helen Maria Williams. It is probable that this was the first copy of this hymn that had reached America. It had certainly never been adopted or used in public worship. Very soon after his return, Mr. Buckminster, whose knowledge of music was as thorough as his love of it was ardent, in conjunction, says tradition, with Hon. Nahum Mitchell and Bartholomew Brown, Esq., altered a piece of Pleyel's instrumental music, adapting it to the hymn, and the two were sung for the first time in this country at Brattle-Street Church, in the autumn of 1807. Wedded together then and there, the union has been so universally recognized and approved for nearly seventy years, that any attempt at divorce is immediately condemned. Few congregations would be pleased at hearing that hymn sung to any but this tune, which was at first called "Hymn Second," and once published under the name of "Bengal," but was soon, —as early as 1811, — in honor of Mr. Buckminster and the church where it was first sung, called "Brattle Street," and is now universally known and designated by that name.

THE NEW

BRATTLE-SQUARE CHURCH.

Laying the Corner Stone.

THE corner-stone of the new Brattle-Square Church, corner of Commonwealth Avenue and Clarendon Street, was laid on Thursday, September 14, with simple but appropriate and interesting services, which opened with the reading of some passages of Scripture and prayer by the Rev. Dr. LOTHROP. Mr. JOHN GARDNER, chairman of the Building Committee, then read the following

REPORT OF THE COMMITTEE.

It is a pleasure to meet on this occasion to lay the corner-stone of the new Brattle-Square Church, and place within it some historical records of the church and society, whose origin dates back to 1699, one hundred and seventy-three years ago.

It is not necessary for me to name the eminent, learned, and pious men who have so successfully preached from its pulpit. History bears evidence to the great and good work done by each in his day and generation. Perhaps, also, no Christian society in the land has counted among its members from time to time so great a number of eminent statesmen, whose influence throughout the whole country did so much to mould public opinion, and establish the republican government under which we now live.

Governor Hancock and Governor Bowdoin were both worshippers at Brattle Square, were liberal contributors towards its support, and large donors towards the erection in 1772 of the edifice that has just been sold. At later periods, the Presidents, John Adams and John Quincy Adams; the celebrated lawyers, Samuel Dexter, Harrison Gray Otis, Daniel Webster, Chief Justice Parker, Judge Peter Oxembridge Thacher, and James T. Austin; Drs. John and J. C. Warren, the brothers Sullivan, Gen. Dearborn, Alexander Everett, Benjamin Crowninshield; also many liberal, distinguished and influential merchants, Thomas Russell, Theodore Lyman, Henderson Inches, William, Amos, and Abbott Lawrence, as well as many others that might be mentioned, were at some time proprietors and worshippers at Brattle-Square Church.

The idea was expressed by Dr. Palfrey, in his sermon preached at the installation of our much-respected pastor, " You must bear in mind that what you preach from this desk will be heard by those whose positions in the councils of the nation will take the sentiments uttered here and disseminate them throughout the wide domain of the country."

Some five years since it became apparent that the location of the church in Brattle Square, surrounded as it was by the encroaching demands of trade and commerce, was no longer adapted to the wants or convenience of the society, and that some new location nearer the homes of its members, and more agreeable of access, must be sought and obtained. At that time the lot we now stand on was purchased by some members of the parish with the purpose of offering it at the low price paid for it to the society, whenever it should vote to remove. No better spot, we think, could then or since have been secured. Its prominence from every point of view, its central position on this broad avenue, its proximity to the increasing population in this southern and western part of the city, and its short distance from Beacon Hill, commend the site as a good selection. It will soon be surrounded by the residences of a population of nearly one hundred thousand.

The committee appointed by the society, when fully authorized to sell the church and property in Brattle Square and erect a suitable church on some more commodious spot, decided at once to accept this lot from the parishioners, who had purchased and were ready to transfer it by deed to the society.

The church property in Brattle Street is sold. Contracts were made some months since for the erection of this structure, which is being built in the Norman-Lombardic style of architecture, and of materials such as you see before you, — Roxbury stone, and brown sand-stone. Unlike any other church in the city, it will have an imposing tower of about one hundred and ninety feet in height. The cost of the whole land and structure will not be far from the resources we shall have at command. And when we have put this stone with its contents in its place, on that solid foundation under the ponderous tower to be erected, may it rest there for centuries to come, undisturbed by earthquakes, revolutions, or contending armies. May this temple stand unscathed, save by the hand of time, and from its altar may there go forth all good influences and religious instructions, teaching love to one another, adoration of God, and love for our Redeemer, till time shall be no more.

At the close of his remarks, Mr. Gardner enumerated the contents of the sealed box, which were as follows : —

The *Daily Advertiser*, of July 31, 1871, containing the sermon by Rev. Dr. Lothrop, the minister of the church, on the 30th of July, being the last service held in the church in Brattle Square.

A history of the church and society, written by Rev. S. K. Lothrop, published in 1851.

Charter granted by the legislature in 1822, with a list of the ministers of the church from 1698, with the by-laws of the church.

Charter granted by the legislature in 1871.

Copies of the following papers : *Daily Advertiser*, dated September 14, 1871 ; Boston *Morning Post* and *Weekly*, September 14, 1871 ; Boston *Journal*, September 14, 1871 ; Boston *Evening Transcript*, September 13 and 14, 1871, and *Weekly;* Boston *Evening Traveller*, September 14 ; Boston *Christian Register*, September 9 ; New York *Liberal Christian*, September 9.

Photographs of the pastor and several others.
Copper cent of 1803 ; copper cent of 1715 ; silver six-cent piece, of
Philip V. of Spain, 1737. These coins were found on the premises
of the old church.

The box was then set with cement in the proposed
cavity by Dr. Lothrop, assisted by the chairman of the
Building Committee and the contracting mason, Mr.
Augustus Lothrop ; and the corner-stone was lowered
into its place. The anthem, " God is a Spirit," was then
· sung ; after which, Dr. Lothrop delivered the following
address : —

My Christian Friends, and especially Members and Repre-
sentatives of the Society recently worshipping in Brattle
Square, —

The chairman of the Building Committee, Mr.
Gardner, at the opening of this service stated to you
its purpose. That purpose has now been substan-
tially accomplished. He, in conjunction with his associates on the committee, and myself as pastor (in the
regretted absence of our deacon, Mr. P. T. Homer, to
whom this service was assigned), have just laid the
corner-stone of our new church, depositing within and
beneath it a box (whose contents have been stated), to
remain there unseen by mortal eyes, until in the providence of God and the progress of time this church, too,
shall have fulfilled its mission, and receive its mandate to
depart. The occasion has a meaning and significance,
lessons of duty and of hope. It awakens memories,
enforces obligations, is an expression of feelings, principles, purposes, which are swelling in all our hearts,
but which it is not necessary I should undertake here
and now fully to set forth. Let me simply say that, as
a religious society, we gather here to-day as pilgrims
and strangers, without house or home, seeking to lay the

foundations, to build here the walls of a new habitation, a new religious home, for ourselves, our families, and the generations who may come after us. Even as our Fathers, of glorious and blessed memory — the Pilgrims of 1620, '30, and '34 — at the sacrifice of many sacred associations and tender affections, in the spirit of a devout faith, at the call of conscience and duty, tore themselves away, turned their backs upon the dear old churches, the sacred spots and happy homes of England, and came over to this land, to build here new churches and new homes, and to worship and serve God under broader and fairer opportunities, — so we have given our hearts a terrible wrench, our memories and affections a painful shock; we have abandoned, torn ourselves away from a noble old church, — grand, solemn, imposing in itself, but so surrounded, pressed upon, buried, as it were, beneath the gathering accumulations of the world in its growing business and enterprise, as to have lost those properties of convenience and invitation which should mark a church, — we have torn ourselves away from this, — at what pain, none but those of us who have done it can estimate, — and come down here to this new and more open spot, that we may build here a new house of worship, establish here a new religious home, enshrine in it all the memories of the past, embark and intrust to it all the hopes of the future, and, in it and through it, give to our religious organization, and to the freedom and simplicity of that Congregational faith and worship it aims to uphold, a fairer and broader opportunity to grow and expand, to exert more and more its beneficent influence as a permanent and pervading power in this community.

My friends, I rejoice, — but knowing most of you, your Christian sentiments and spirit, so well as I do, I may use the plural number, and say we, — we all rejoice in the religious liberty enjoyed in our country, where each and

all are free to worship God according to the dictates of
their consciences. We rejoice in every token of a living
faith and earnest zeal displayed by any of the denomina-
tions of Christian men and women that compose our
community. We rejoice in every indication, no matter
by whom made, that God is recognized and worshipped,
Christ received, reverenced, obeyed, and his Gospel
made the inspiration and law of life to the soul. And, as
we stand here to-day, in this southern and western part
of our growing city, and look around upon its increasing
number of new churches, — upon those whose spires,
pointing towards heaven, show that they are already
completed, and upon those whose foundations are just
begun, — as we look around upon them all, from the
majestic and massive Cathedral of the Roman Catholic
to the church whose corner-stone was laid yesterday, we
bid them all God speed. May they all be fountains of
living waters to them that drink thereat. May they all
redound to the glory of God, the honor of Christ, and
the good of man. May they all stand for the defence
and furtherance of Christian light and love, holiness and
truth, for the regeneration of the world and the salvation of souls. We would come among them, not in the
spirit of opposition, or a narrow, sectarian bigotry, but in
the spirit of Christian respect and sympathy, to strive by
competing in love and zeal to promote the highest and
best interests, the coming of the kingdom of God in
this community. But, while we thus embrace all with
a broad catholic charity, and desire to live in peace with
all, we cleave closest, we love deepest, we respect most
profoundly, we give faith, heart, conscience, and our
best service to that simple, free, independent Congrega-
tionalism which we have received from our Fathers;
which, as a form of Gospel administration, was the
pristine glory of New England; to which she owes so

much that is honorable in her history and noble in her character; to which the ancestors of so many of us were martyrs and servants in England and in this country; and which, as we read and interpret the New Testament, corresponds, in organization, form, and service, more nearly than any other to those primitive Christian churches, which Paul and the apostles planted around the shores of the eastern Mediterranean, in the first century of the Christian era. We are sad when any one of these old Congregational churches dies out, becomes extinct. We rejoice when any one of them is spiritually renovated, imbued with fresh life, placed (as we are endeavoring to place ours) in a position to prolong its existence, and increase its power, and become more and more a living church of the Lord Jesus Christ. It is therefore, brethren, and ought to be, in gladness and gratitude that we meet here to-day, and, with prayer and supplication, lay the corner-stone of our new church. From this hour let sacred associations and interests begin to gather in our hearts around this spot, leading us to forget the things that are behind and press forward to those that are before, — forget them so far as their memory would be a clog to our zeal, a hindrance to our efforts, a palsy upon our energy; remember them only to make them an inspiration to faith, hope, courage, to every thing demanded of us to carry forward to completion the goodly Christian work we have undertaken, and have here and now asked God to bless. Let us so remember the past and so embrace the future that both may quicken and invigorate our fidelity.

Brethren, the independent Congregational Church — the "manifesto" church of 1699 which has come down to us by inheritance and descent, and which we here represent, — in its history, character, principles is worthy of our regard and our devoted service. It combines and harmonizes, to as great an extent as is practicable, the principles of authority and freedom ; maintaining, as a body or religious society, its own independence of all external authority by its subjection to the Master in his great revelation, and securing the freedom of every individual member of the body in the interpretation of that revelation. The great declaration of its covenant is, "We believe in one God, the Father Almighty, Maker of heaven and earth ; and in Jesus Christ as the promised Messiah and Saviour of the world ; and receive the holy Scriptures as a revelation of the mind and will of God to men for their salvation." The great demand — the simple, grand, comprehensive demand — which it makes upon every one who would join in its service at the table of Communion is one that recognizes liberty and supposes progress. "Will you endeavor to yield obedience to every truth of God that has been or shall be made known to *you* as *your* duty, the Lord assisting you by his Spirit and grace?" It is because we believe these declarations and principles to be the spiritual corner-stones of the spiritual Church of Christ, that we seek to transplant them from the original spot where our Fathers embodied them in temple and worship to this new spot, that here they may take fresh root, spring up strong and fruitful, and in the future, as in the past, nourish the spiritual life of many generations. Let us prosecute this work, so happily begun, with a zeal and fidelity worthy of its character and importance ; and may God continue to bless it with the smiles of his favor. May this church go steadily forward to completion without delay or accident, or loss of life or limb to any engaged in erecting it. When it stands finished throughout from its firm foundations to the capstones of its lofty tower, may the blessed Providence permit us to gather here with devout and grateful hearts, and, in the spirit of a holy faith, consecrate it to the worship of the one God, the Father Almighty ; to the honor and service of his only begotten Son, the Lord Jesus Christ. And, so long as its walls shall stand, and men and women gather in it for worship, in Christian faith and trust, may the Father and the Son make it the scene and the channel through which to shed down, in rich abundance, those influences of the Holy Spirit which are for the consolation, the enlightenment and redemption of the world ; and may we, brethren, when we come to worship within these walls, and may all who come after us, see to it that, through these influences of the Holy Spirit and our own efforts and prayers, the spiritual temple of a holy Christian character — more glorious and beautiful than any outward temple, — be built up in our hearts.

www.ingramcontent.com/pod-product-compliance
Lightning Source LLC
Chambersburg PA
CBHW022035080426
42733CB00007B/834